D0889950

KARATE

Rennay Craats

Weigl Publishers Inc.

Published by Weigl Publishers Inc.
123 South Broad Street, Box 227
Mankato, MN 56002
USA
Copyright © 2002 Weigl Publishers Inc.
Web site: www.weigl.com

All rights reserved. No part of this publication
may be reproduced, stored in a retrieval system, or
transmitted in any form or by any means, electronic,
mechanical, photocopying, recording, or otherwise,
without the prior written permission of Weigl
Publishers Inc.

Library of Congress Cataloging-in-Publication
Data available upon request from the publisher.
Fax: (507) 388-2746 for the attention of the
Publishing Records Department.
ISBN: 1-930954-17-4

Printed in the United States of America
1 2 3 4 5 6 7 8 9 05 04 03 02 01

Managing Editor
Kara Turner
Layout and Design
Warren Clark
Terry Paulhus
Susan Kenyon
Copy Editor
Jennifer Nault

Photograph credits
Cover: Corbis Images; Corbis Images: page 1, 3, 4,
5L, 7B, 8, 11, 13L, 14, 15L, 18, 19, 21, 23; Eyewire:
page 20L; PhotoDisc Ltd: page 20R; Sporting Images
Australia: page 5R, 6, 7T, 10, 12L, 12R, 13R, 15R,
16L, 16R, 17.

Every reasonable effort
has been made to trace
ownership and to obtain
permission to reprint
copyright material.
The publishers would be
pleased to have any errors
or omissions brought to
their attention so that
they may be corrected
in subsequent printings.

Contents

What is Karate?

Karate is a martial art that began in China in the sixth century. Although no one is sure, it was likely introduced by an Indian monk named Bodhidharma. He noticed that his monks had become thin and weak. They spent all their time praying. Bodhidharma taught them ways to strengthen and control their bodies through breathing and stretching. Much later, in 1914, Japanese master Gichin Funakoshi used aspects of this old form to create another one. He demonstrated it to martial arts experts in Tokyo, Japan, in 1922. The experts were so impressed, they asked him to stay and teach. His martial art was called *karate-do*, which means "the way of the empty hand."

Karate first came to the U.S. in the 1940s. Other forms made their way into martial arts studios in the 1950s and 1960s.

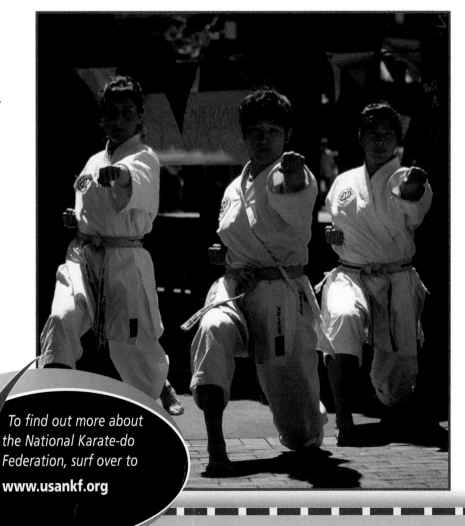

CHECK IT OUT

To find out more about the National Karate-do Federation, surf over to **www.usankf.org**

There are many different forms of karate. These forms are from Japan, Korea, and China and are all closely related. Japanese forms use simple movements. Korean forms feature combinations of movements, especially kick combinations. Chinese movements are more smooth and flowing, unlike the sharp and choppy moves of the other forms. Different instructors teach different forms of the art.

Karate is related to other martial arts, such as **judo** and **jujitsu**. Unlike those sports, karate concentrates on kicking and punching rather than wrestling. People who practice karate often spar, or compete, against each other. They also focus on form, or *kata*. A kata is a demonstration of karate skills and techniques. There are many different kata.

More than 200 Japanese terms are used for the various blows and moves in karate.

Karate has been incorporated in training programs for soldiers, police officers, and college athletes.

Getting Ready to Play

To practice karate, students need only a loose, comfortable pair of sweat pants and a T-shirt. Dressing for lessons and competitions is another story. A karate *gi* is worn during classes and tournaments. A gi is most commonly made of white cotton canvas. Students are expected to take care of their gis as a sign of respect. They wash them every time they are used to keep them crisp and clean.

A gi jacket wraps around the body. The left side wraps over the right and is tied at the right side. Gis are usually white. A student may sew a patch on the jacket to show where he or she trains.

A belt wraps around the student's waist twice and is tied in a knot at the front. The color of the belt shows the trainee's level. The levels below black belt are called *kyu* grades.

Traditional gi pants are fastened with drawstrings. Non-traditional gis feature elastic waistbands or lace-up pants.

To become masters of karate, students use many different pieces of equipment in their training. For example, a punching board is used to practice strikes. It helps develop strong hands. A speed bag develops timing and coordination. Karate students kick and punch this piece of equipment. Heavy bags, such as those used in boxing, help trainees become more powerful attackers. Punches and kicks are practiced with heavy bags. Kicking balls are hung in many karate *dojos,* or studios. They are used to improve the trainee's jumping ability. They also develop the coordination needed for flying kicks.

The black belt is the highest level of karate. It is subdivided into ranks called *dan*. First dan black belts learn advanced moves and may teach young students. Karate students continue to advance through levels until they are masters or grand masters. This takes many years to achieve.

Advanced karate students use kicking boards to strengthen their feet.

The Karate Dojo

When students enter and leave the dojo, they bow. This is to show respect for the sport, the founding master of their school, and their instructors, called **sensei**. Most dojos have mirrors on all the walls. This allows karate students to watch themselves to make sure they are using proper form and technique.

Many other martial arts dojos have rubber or foam mats on the floor. This prevents injuries when students are thrown. As karate is a sport of punches and kicks, mats are not necessary. Karate dojos have a wooden floor like that in a school gymnasium.

At the beginning and end of each class, students line up and make a formal bow to their sensei.

Karate students use a flat surface to perform their kata. There is no set size for this area. It must be large enough for the athletes to complete their routines without running out of room. For sparring competitions, or **kumite**, an area of about 26 feet by 26 feet is set aside. The boundaries are clearly marked with thick lines. Strips of tape in the center of the square are often used to show where each competitor starts.

The referee gives the signal to start and stop a kumite by calling "*yame.*"

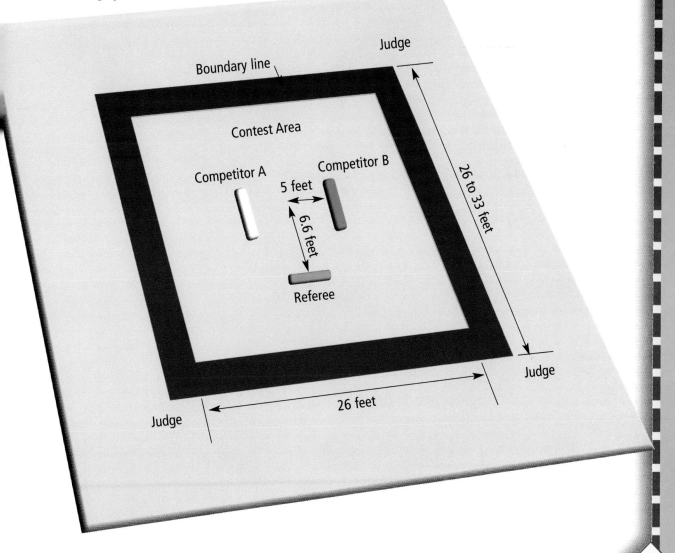

Judge

Boundary line

Contest Area

Competitor A   Competitor B

5 feet

6.6 feet

Referee

26 to 33 feet

Judge

26 feet

Judge

Rules of Competition

A kumite lasts for 3 minutes for men and 2 minutes for women and juniors, or until someone scores three points. Young competitors do not actually hit their opponents. They stop their kicks and punches 1 inch from their opponent's body. Students need to learn this control in order to advance. In older divisions, light contact is allowed. If no one scores three points by the end of the match, the competitor with the most points is the winner. If there is a tie or neither competitor scores, they continue sparring. The first one to score a point wins.

Tori, the attacker, must land a punch or kick in the target areas to score. The targets are the head, chest, stomach, and back. The attack must be focused and controlled to earn a point. *Uke*, the defender, tries to block the strikes to prevent his or her opponent from scoring a point.

As karate involves kicking and punching, many students wear hand and foot gloves. A mouth guard is another useful piece of safety equipment.

During karate competitions, the rules must be followed. Judges can choose to warn an offender or give penalty points if a rule is broken. Judges want to keep the match safe. Competitors need to stay within the boundary lines or risk a penalty. If a player uses moves that are not allowed or uses too much force in his or her attacks, a penalty is given. A judge can **disqualify** a competitor for trying to hurt an opponent or for disobeying the rules.

There are usually three judges and a referee overseeing a karate match. The referee follows the action in the middle while the judges watch the corners of the square. The judges decide when a point is earned. They raise one finger and point at the scorer with the other hand. To show that an attack does not earn points, the judges cross their arms downward.

If a competitor shows disrespect to the judges or another competitor, his or her opponent is awarded a point.

CHECK IT OUT

Learn more about the rules of karate at
www.karate-online.de/wkfrules.htm

11

Learning the Moves

Before karate students learn kicks or punches, they learn stances. Many karate stances give maximum stability, yet also allow for easy movement. The *zenkutsu dachi*, or front stance, is the first stance students learn. It has students in a slightly lunged position. This gives students power and balance when they are moving forward with their kicks and strikes. In the back stance, *kokutsu dachi*, students have most of their weight on the back leg.

Karate students are expected to train with their sensei at least twice a week.

Karate students learn good posture and balance as part of their training in stances.

A s karate is a self-defense art, learning to block attacks is very important. In the beginning, students perform the blocks slowly. This allows them to learn proper technique. Once the motion feels natural, they speed it up to defend themselves against actual attacks. Students often use rigid arm swings to block a kick or a punch. Different techniques are used to protect different parts of the body and shield against different methods of attack. High blocks are used to protect the head, and middle blocks are used to protect the chest and stomach. Low blocks are completed in a wide stance. These blocks defend attacks to the mid-section and lower body. Some blocks can even defend against two attacks at once.

The three key elements in karate are speed, strength, and technique.

Punches and blocks are usually practiced with a partner.

Strikes and Kicks

Strikes are blows delivered using the hands and arms. This includes punching, elbowing, and chopping. Karate punches are different from boxing ones. In karate, the force of the punch is focused on the first two knuckles of the fist. This gives the strike more power. Also, karate punches are thrown without moving the shoulder or body. Students need to keep their backs straight at all times. There are many variations of karate punches that depend on the stance and the position of the arms.

The karate chop is a powerful offensive weapon. Students have to make sure they do not make contact with the side of their fingers. This could cause injuries. Instead, they make contact on the area between the wrist and the little finger.

One of the first lessons in karate is that good balance gives karate punches extra power.

Kicking is an exciting part of karate. The front kick is the basic kick in the sport. The toes are curled back, and the ball of the foot hits the target. Students lift their knee straight up and then snap their foot forward. Other kicks use this basic movement. Side kicks snap the foot out to the student's side. This kick can be aimed at the knees or chest. The roundhouse is a popular and powerful kick. Students balance on one leg and raise the other leg behind their hip. The kick then travels in an arc toward the opponent's head or body.

The roundhouse kick is one of the most spectacular karate moves.

Beginners often find training in kicking hard work.

CHECK IT OUT

To learn more about karate kicks, head to

www.fac.swt.edu/ Beginning%20Karate/k040.html

Competing in Karate

Many children begin learning karate at a young age. Karate classes often last for 1 or 2 hours. During lessons, students practice each move under the watchful eye of their sensei. As they improve and learn more moves, students advance to higher belt levels.

Many people enjoy meeting karate students from other places who love the sport as much as they do. Tournaments are a good place to do this. Students can compete in kumite or enter kata competitions.

After the age of 12, competitors are no longer grouped by age or size. They are grouped by rank instead.

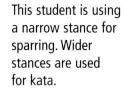

This student is using a narrow stance for sparring. Wider stances are used for kata.

As karate students advance, they can try out for state, regional, or national teams. These teams enter highly competitive tournaments. They compete against the best karate students in competitions around the world. Some martial arts are official events at the Olympic Games, but karate is not one of them. Karate has many different branches with different sets of rules. Some people argue that it would be difficult to include a general karate event at the Olympics. However, many organizations around the world would like to see karate declared an Olympic event. Until then, athletes may compete in regional, national, and world championships.

Among the best-known competitions in the U.S. are the annual American Championships of the Japan Karate Association, and the All-American Open Karate Championships.

CHECK IT OUT

To find out more about world competitions, surf to

www.wkf.net

Traditions of the Sport

As is the case with other martial arts, traditions are very important in karate. One of these traditions is **meditation**. Students sit with their eyes closed and do not move or speak. They relax and clear their minds so they can focus on learning karate.

Another tradition is the *kiai*. The kiai is a sharp yell that shows effort, determination, and concentration. Karate masters noticed that people grunt or exhale when lifting something heavy. They experimented with this idea. They found that forcing air out helps focus strength and energy. The kiai also tightens the stomach muscles. This gives the student more power and strength.

The traditions of karate are very old. Following these traditions is a sign of respect for the sport.

K arate students are expected to give their maximum effort during classes and in competitions. Students are taught **self-discipline**. Many karate students also learn a karate **oath**, called the "*dojo kun*." The oath does not only apply to the sport. It also applies to students' lives away from karate. Here is an example of a dojo kun:

1. Seek perfection of character
2. Be faithful
3. Endeavor
4. Respect others
5. Refrain from violent behavior

Students from several dojos sometimes practice karate together.

Classes often either begin or end with the oath. Students memorize the verse and say it together.

Healthy Living

Karate training is hard work. Students need to keep their bodies strong and healthy in order to stay fit. A balanced diet is a great way to stay healthy. Eating fresh fruit and vegetables, milk and milk products, meats, breads, cereals, grains, and pastas helps keep athletes functioning at their best. Staying stocked up with all the necessary vitamins and minerals will also help their bodies fight sickness. Drinking plenty of water before, during, and after training or competing is also important. Athletes need to replace the water and salts they lose through sweating.

Athletes should hold each stretch for 15 seconds.

One banana has 16 percent of the fiber, 15 percent of the vitamin C, and 11 percent of the potassium athletes need every day for good health.

Karate is a sport of balance and strength. Students need to work to improve in both areas. Warming up is essential. Karate students need to stretch their muscles to improve **flexibility**. Flexible students find it easier to punch and kick. Warmup exercises include arm swings, body bends, toe touches, and lunges. Some karate students use the splits to stretch their legs! Stretching helps get athletes ready to practice. Warming up helps prevent injury and improves athletes' ability to do karate.

The most flexible karate students kick the highest.

CHECK IT OUT

Find out more about eating right at
www.exhibits.pacsci.org/nutrition

Brain Teasers

How much do you know about karate? See if you can answer these questions!

Q How do sand, rice, and gravel help students train in karate?

A Delivering strikes or kicks can hurt at first. Students can drive their hands and feet into boxes of sand, rice, or gravel to toughen them up. Hitting and kicking punching boards or sand bags also toughens the hands and feet.

Q What is the *shuto uchi* more commonly known as?

A It is often called the "karate chop." It is a strike using the edge of the hand.

Q What are "bulls," "bouncers," and "chargers"?

A Bulls are powerful karate competitors who never back down. They are hard to move during attacks. Bouncers are very fast competitors. They strike quickly and move away before their opponents can strike back. Chargers move aggressively at their opponents. They throw many punches and kicks very quickly.

Q How would learning to speak Japanese help a karate student?

A There are hundreds of moves, all of which have Japanese names. Early in the lessons, students learn to count in Japanese. Sensei will call out Japanese numbers when doing drills or certain exercises. Students need to understand in order to follow along.

Q Why must competitors use only light contact during karate competitions?

A The blows learned in karate are very powerful. They can kill another person if they are delivered with full force. To keep competitors safe, students must either stop just short of contact or use only limited contact.

Q Are weapons used in karate?

A While weapons are not really a part of the art, some weapons have been added. These include the nunchaku, the bo staff, and the tonfa. These weapons were all originally Japanese farm tools. Weapons can be very dangerous to use without training. They can easily hurt or kill an opponent.

Glossary

disqualify: disallow from competing because of a violation of the rules

flexibility: the ability to bend and stretch the body easily

judo: a martial art in which throwing and grabbing are important

jujitsu: a martial art in which players hit each other with their hands, feet, and elbows

kumite (pronounced koo-mah-tay): a sparring competition between students of the same rank and often the same gender and size

meditation: deep thought

oath: a serious promise

self-discipline: self-control

sensei: karate master and teacher

tori: the offensive person; the one kicking and striking

uke: the defensive person; the one blocking attacks

Index

Web Sites

www.usankf.org

www.wkf.net

www.karate-online.de/wkfrules.htm

www.exhibits.pacsci.org/nutrition

www.fac.swt.edu/Beginning%20Karate/k040.html